Floral Breakfast

Materials

- 1 (White) 12" rectangular basket without a top handle.
- Floral foam
- Sphagnum moss
- Floral pins
- 10 Stems (orchid) larkspur
- 6 (Purple) medium hydrangeas
- 5 (pink) peonies (3 flowers each)

Tools

- Wire cutters
- Yard stick

Note: Line the basket with newspaper before adding the foam and moss to avoid littering the table with bits of moss when the arrangement is complete.

Instructions

1 Fill the basket with foam all the way to the top. Cover the foam with moss and secure the moss with floral pins.

2 Cut eight larkspur to 15" and insert in foam. Cut the last two larkspur to 13" and insert in the center of the foam.

3 Cut all the hydrangea stems to 10" and place in-between the larkspur.

4 Cut the peony blooms to 13" and place one on each side hanging slightly over the edge of the basket. Cut the remaining peonies to 10" and distribute them evenly through-out the arrangement filling in any empty spaces.

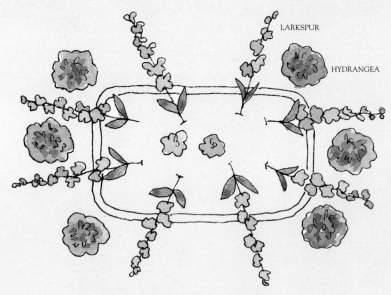

LARKSPUR

HYDRANGEA

TOP VIEW SHOWING POSITION OF LARKSPUR AND HYDRANGEA.

Rose Basket

Materials

- 1 (French blue) 8" round rattan basket with handle
- Floral foam
- Sphagnum moss
- 9 Stems (light pink) roses
- 4 Stems (pink) wild roses (2 flowers each)
- 1 Stem (blue) September flower (3 flowers each)

Tools

- Wire cutters
- Yard stick
- Hot glue gun/glue sticks
- Serrated knife

Note: Hot glue stem tips before inserting into foam for a permanent arrangement.

Instructions

1 Cut foam to fit snugly in basket. Cover with moss.

2 Cut one rose stem to 8" and insert in the center of the basket. Cut the remaining rose stems to 6" and insert in a circle around the first rose. Save the leaves.

TOP VIEW SHOWING POSITION OF ROSES

3 Hot glue three rose leaves facing different directions around each rose.

4 Cut the wild rose stems to 5" and insert a single bloom in-between each of the roses.

5 Cut the September flowers into 5" sections and distribute throughout the arrangement.

Bow Basket

Materials

- *1 (Rose) 8" wall basket with handle*
- *1-2/3 Yards (tapestry) #40 cotton wired ribbon*

Tools

- *Scissors*
- *Yard stick*
- *Hot glue gun/glue sticks*

1 Cut a 20" length of ribbon. Wrap it around the basket and hot glue it to the back. Put a few drops of hot glue on the front center of the ribbon and pinch it together.

Instructions

2 Tie a simple bow with the remaining ribbon and hot glue it to the pinched part of ribbon in the front.

1. MAKE LOOPS TO THE LEFT AND RIGHT LEAVING ENOUGH EXTRA RIBBON FOR THE FIRST TAIL.

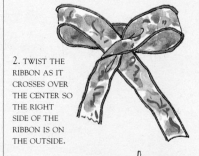

2. TWIST THE RIBBON AS IT CROSSES OVER THE CENTER SO THE RIGHT SIDE OF THE RIBBON IS ON THE OUTSIDE.

3. MAKE A SMALL CENTER LOOP AND TIE WITH WIRE THROUGH LOOP AND AROUND BACK.

4. CUT INVERTED "V" IN TAIL ENDS.

3 Trim the tails to the desired length and shape the bow.

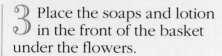

Materials

- 1 (Light green) 6" rectangular basket with handle
- Floral foam
- 6 Ounces (natural) excelsior
- 5 Stems (peach) ranunculus (2 flowers each)
- 4 Stems (lavender) tweedia
- 2 Yards 1-3/4" (Pink/white) wired ribbon
- 4 (peach) guest soaps
- 1 (peach) lotion
- 1 (peach) boxed soap leaves
- Floral wire

Tools

- Serrated knife
- Yard stick
- Wire cutters

Instructions

1. Wedge the foam inside the basket and cover it with excelsior.

2. Cut one ranunculus stem to 11", one stem to 9" and the rest to 8". Insert the tallest stem in the middle on the right side of the handle.

   Insert the 9" stem in front of it on the left side of the handle. Fill in the arrangement on both sides with the remaining ranunculi.

3. Place the soaps and lotion in the front of the basket under the flowers.

4. Cut the tweedia stems to 6" and insert in-between the ranunculi and the soaps etc.

5. Make a 7" wide, 6 loop graduated bow with a center loop and 5" tails. Secure the center with floral wire and wire it to the base of the handle. Fluff out the loops and cut the tails in "v's"

Rose Parade

Materials

- 1 (Natural) 6' grapevine garland
- 12 Stems (rose) large open roses
- 8 Stems (light pink) wild roses (2 flowers each)

Tools

- Wire cutters
- Hot glue gun/glue sticks

Instructions

1 Cut the rose stems to 1/2", and hot glue the blooms to the garland equally spaced. Hot glue 3-4 rose leaves around every rose.

2 Cut the wild rose stems to 5", and hot glue each stem in-between the roses.

Moody Blooms

Materials

- 1 (Green) 12" rectangular basket with handle
- Floral foam
- Sphagnum moss
- Floral pins
- 6 Stems (dark green) Magnolia branches
- 8 Stems (mauve) hydrangeas

Tools

- Wire cutters
- Yard stick

Instructions

1 Wedge enough foam in the basket to rise 1" above the rim. Cover the foam with moss, and secure the moss with floral pins.

2 Cut the magnolia leaves into 12" sections. Insert in foam evenly spaced, extending out the sides and over the top of the handle.

3 Cut the hydrangea stems to 12" and distribute throughout the leaves.

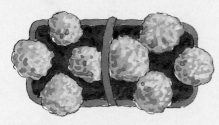

TOP VIEW SHOWING POSITION OF HYDRANGEAS.

Tumbling Floral Spice

Materials

- 1 (Natural) 6" round basket with handle
- 1 (Natural) 4" round basket with handle
- Floral foam
- Sphagnum moss
- Floral pins
- 5 (Natural) large garlic heads
- 7 Stems (yellow) medium sunflowers
- 36 (Red) small chili peppers
- 11 (Green) brussel sprouts
- Floral wire

Note: The garlic, chilis and sprouts can be preserved or silk

Tools

- Serrated knife
- Wire cutters
- Yard stick
- Hot glue gun/glue sticks

Instructions

1 Wire the two baskets together. Hot glue to secure position.

2 Hot glue a 2" cube of foam to the inside of the small basket, and wedge a piece of foam in the large basket. Cover the pieces of foam with moss and secure the moss with floral pins.

3 Run pieces of floral wire through the top of each garlic head. Cut the wire to 4" and insert it into the foam. Put one in the small basket and four across the center of the large basket.

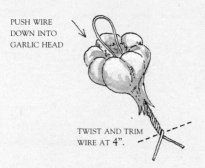

PUSH WIRE DOWN INTO GARLIC HEAD

TWIST AND TRIM WIRE AT 4".

4 Cut the sunflower stems to 6". Insert two in the small basket and five in the large basket in-between and around the garlic. Hot glue two sunflower leaves around every flower.

5 Hot glue the peppers all over the basket in-between the sunflowers and garlic.

6 Hot glue or wire three sprouts in the small basket and eight in the large basket. Fill in any empty spaces.

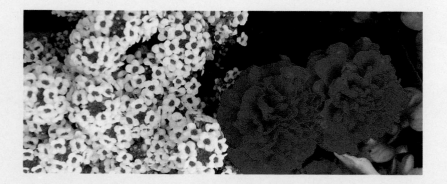

Pink Splendor

Materials

- 1 (Willow and birch) 12" rectangular basket with handle
- Floral foam
- Sphagnum moss
- Floral pins
- 11 Stems (rose) delphinium
- 6 Stems (pink) medium peonies
- 6 Stems (purple) small alliums
- 8 Stems (purple) cosmos (4 flowers each)
- 4 Stems (rose) bouvardia (3 flowers each)
- 12 Stems (pink) larkspur

Tools

- Wire cutters
- Yard stick

Instructions

1 Wedge the foam in the basket and cover it with moss. Secure the moss with floral pins.

2 Cut one delphinium stem to 20", and insert it in the center of the basket. Cut the remaining delphinium stems to 17", and establish the overall shape of the arrangement.

TOP VIEW SHOWING PLACEMENT OF DELPHINIUMS.

3 Cut the peony stems to 14" and fill in around the delphiniums.

4 Cut four allium stems to 11" and place one in each corner of the arrangement. Cut two allium stems to 16" and place one top center right and one top center left.

5 Cut all the cosmos stems to 16" and fill in the arrangement.

6 Cut the bouvardia into 12" single stems and fill in any empty spaces.

7 Cut the larkspur stems to 6" and place next to the delphiniums.

Texas Roses

Materials

- 1 (Dark) 15" rectangular basket with handle
- Floral foam
- Sphagnum moss
- Floral pins
- 7 Stems (yellow) large rose buds
- 8 Stems (yellow) 1/2 open large roses
- 6 Stems (yellow) open large roses
- 3 1/2 Yards (ivory) #9 French wired ribbon
- Floral wire

Tools

- Wire cutters
- Yard stick
- Scissors

Instructions

1 Wedge the foam in the basket and cover it with moss. Secure the moss with floral pins.

2 Cut three rose bud stems to 22, 20, and 18". Cut three half open roses to 13, 12, and 11". Cut two open blooms to 10". Insert the buds in the back left of the basket, the half open blooms under the buds and the open blooms between the half open roses and over the rim of the basket.

NUMBERS INSIDE FLOWERS SHOW LENGTH OF STEM IN INCHES.

3 Cut two bud stems to 13", one half open rose to 18" and three open roses to 16, 12, and 10". Insert as shown.

4 Cut one open rose stem to 12", four half open roses to 12", one bud to 17" and the remaining bud stem to 7" Insert in foam.

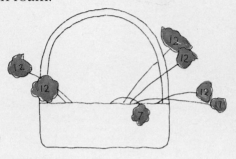

5 Add any remaining foliage in-between the roses.

6 Cut 1-1/2 yards from the ribbon and weave it from the upper left side of the arrangement down around the front to the right side. Make a bow with the remaining ribbon. Secure it with a 7" floral wire and insert the wire into the foam, in the front on the left.

Hot Poppies

Materials

- 1 (Bronze) 8" square basket
- Floral foam
- Sphagnum moss
- Floral pins
- 1 Bush (green) geranium leaves (20 stems)
- 10 Stems (red) poppies
- 3 Stems (red) chili peppers

Tools

- Wire cutters
- Yard stick

Instructions

1 Wedge the foam in the basket and cover it with moss. Secure the moss with floral pins.

2 Insert the geranium bush in the center of the foam. Open up all the leaves and arrange the shape of the greenery.

3 Cut the poppy stems to 21, 18, 15, 14, 13, 12, 11, 11, 11 and 11". Insert the poppies throughout the greenery starting with the tallest stems first.

4 Fill in any holes at the bottom of the arrangement with chili peppers.

Gracious Floral Basket

Materials

- 1 (Natural) 16" rectangular basket with handle
- Floral foam
- Sphagnum moss
- Floral pins
- 8 Stems (fuchsia) phalaenopsis orchid sprays
- 13 (Natural) 3' birch branches
- 11 Stems (cream) large crown peonies (with buds)
- 12 Stems (pink) snapdragons
- 8 Stems (white) cosmos (4 flowers each)

Tools

- Yard stick
- Wire cutters
- Clippers

Instructions

1 Line the bottom of the basket with newspaper. Wedge enough floral foam in the basket to fit snugly. Cover the foam with moss, and secure the moss with floral pins.

2 Cut two orchid stems to 27 and 25", and place them in the center on either side of the handle. Cut six orchid stems to 22" and place one in each of the four corners of the basket and two in the center of the foam.

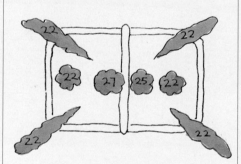

NUMBERS INSIDE ORCHIDS SHOW LENGTH OF STEM IN INCHES.

3 Insert a 3 foot stem of birch in the center of the arrangement. Cut two stems to 26" and insert them on either side of the center one. Cut ten stems to 22" and place one in each of the corners and the remaining stems throughout the arrangement.

4 Cut one peony to 30" and insert it in the center of the foam next to the birch. Cut two stems to 24" and place one in the front and one in the back of the center peony. Cut six stems to 18" and place three on each side, front and back of the center flowers. Cut two stems to 22" and place between the top and side flowers on each side of the arrangement.

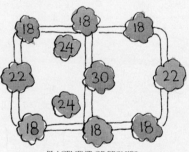

PLACEMENT OF PEONIES

5 Cut four snapdragons to 26" and place them all around the center peonies. Cut eight snapdragons to 22" and place one in each corner, and one on each side of the basket.

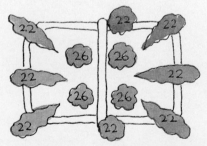

PLACEMENT OF SNAPDRAGONS

6 Cut three cosmos to 24" and place them around the center flowers. Cut the remaining cosmos to 20" and fill in the arrangement.

KITCHEN FRUITS

Materials

- 1 (Natural) 8" round, willow basket with handle
- Floral foam
- Sphagnum moss
- Floral pins
- Plastic:
  - 1 Banana
  - 2 Mini pumpkins
  - 1 Small apple
  - 1 Crook neck squash
  - 1 Pomegranate
  - 1 Pear
  - 2 (Purple) grape clusters
- 1 Silk peach
- 3 Stems (green) ivy
- 2 Stems (pink) alstromeria
- Floral pins

Tools

- Hot glue gun/glue sticks
- Wire cutters
- Yard stick

Instructions

1. Wedge foam into basket and cover it with sphagnum moss. Secure the moss with floral pins.

2. Hot glue the peach to the right side of the basket. Hot glue the squash next to the peach. Hot glue the banana next to the squash and hot glue the apple left of the banana. Hot glue the grapes on top of the banana.

3. Turn the basket around. Hot glue the pear on the right side of the basket. Hot glue the pomegranate under the handle, and hot glue the two squash on the left side of the basket side by side.

4. Cut the ivy into 5" pieces and glue in-between the fruit.

5. Cut the alstromeria stems to 5" and hot glue them in-between the fruit and ivy.

Popular Pansies

Materials

- 1 (Dark) oval 10" basket with handle
- Floral foam
- Sphagnum moss
- Floral pins
- 1 Bush (purple/green) purple passion leaves
- 3 Bushes (lavender) pansies (8 flowers each)
- 1 Bush (green) ivy (15 stems)

Tools

- Wire cutters
- Yard stick

Instructions

1 Wedge foam into the basket and cover it with moss. Secure the moss with floral pins.

2 Cut the ivy bush into separate stems. Wrap the longest stem around the basket handle. Set aside remaining pieces.

3 Insert the purple passion bush into the center of the basket in back of the handle. Arrange the long stems to flow to the right in front and the shorter stems to fill in the back and stand up in the middle. Insert ivy stems to fill in the shape of the leaves.

4 Insert one pansy bush in the back of the basket and spread out the flowers and leaves. Insert the second pansy bush a little left of center in front of the handle. Spread the flowers and leaves. Cut the flowers into single stems from the remaining pansy bush and fill in the arrangement.

French Basket Bouquet

Materials

- 1 (White) 20" fireside basket
- Floral foam
- Sphagnum moss
- Floral pins
- 8 Stems (purple) dendrobium orchids (2 flowers each)
- 8 Stems (orchid/purple) tiger lilies
- 6 Stems (dark purple) anemones (3 flowers each)
- 12 Stems (periwinkle blue) campanula

Tools

- Wire cutters
- Yard stick
- Hot glue gun/glue sticks

Instructions

1. Hot glue the floral foam to the center of the basket. Cover the top and sides with moss. Secure with floral pins.

2. Cut eight orchid stems to 15" and insert in all directions. Add the orchid foliage around the base of some of the blooms.

3. Cut four tiger lily stems to 12" and insert in-between the orchids at the four corners of the foam. Cut the remaining stems to 10" and insert them in-between the orchids near the center of the basket.

4. Cut all the anemone stems to 12". Distribute throughout the arrangement.

5. Cut all the campanula to 13" and insert throughout the basket filling in any empty spaces.

PLACEMENT OF ORCHID STEMS

PLACEMENT OF TIGER LILIES

Peony Power

Materials

- *Your favorite 6" tall, 5" wide vase*
- *Floral foam*
- *Sphagnum moss*
- *Floral pins*
- *5 Stems (pink) large peonies with buds*
- *2 Stems (lavender) cosmos (4 flowers each)*
- *2 Stems (rose) bouvardia (3 flowers each)*

Tools

- *Wire cutters*
- *Yard stick*

Instructions

1. Wedge foam inside vase and cover it with moss. Secure the moss with floral pins.

2. Cut peony stems to 10" and insert in foam facing all directions. (Bend the stems into graceful curves with your thumb and forefingers before inserting.)

3. Cut cosmo stems to 7" and insert in front and in back. Spread the flowers.

4. Cut the bouvardia apart leaving 7-8" stems and fill in the arrangement on all sides.

TOP VIEW SHOWING PLACEMENT OF PEONIES

Wonderful Wall Hanging

Materials

- 5 Stems (pink) 1/2 open roses
- 6 Stems (pink/white) morning glories (2 flowers and bud)
- 6 Stems (purple/green) lilacs
- 3 Stems (yellow) forsythia
- 2 Stems (dark green) palm leaves
- 3 Yards (pink) 2" French wired ribbon
- Floral wire
- Floral tape

Tools

- Yard stick
- Clippers

Note: The ivy leaves at the top of the drapes in the photo on page 33 are not part of the project.

Instructions

1 The project is 4-1/2 ft. long. Lay the palm leaves on a table (or the floor), and lay the forsythia on top. Wire the stems together at the top, and cover the wire with floral tape.

2 Cut three rose stems to 14, 12 and 11". Wire the ends of the stems together and tape them to the fern and forsythia. Tape the fourth rose to the middle of the arrangement and the fifth rose to the end. Fan out the leaves.

3 Add the morning glories following the same procedure as the roses and tape the stems to secure.

4 Add the lilacs, following the same procedure, distributing them evenly throughout the arrangement. Spread the flowers and smooth the leaves.

5 Wrap the ends of the stems at the top using one yard of ribbon. Make a simple bow with 12" tails, 6" from the end.

6 Make a hanging loop out of florist wire and attach it to the back at the top of the arrangement.

Note: This beautiful arrangement of flowers can also be placed on a mantle or draped over a buffet or table. Add a few candles at different heights for charm.

Green Basket/White Flowers

Materials

- 1 (Forest green) 10" oval basket with handle
- Floral foam
- Sphagnum moss
- Floral pins
- 10 Stems (variegated) boxwood sprays
- 4 Stems (white) snowball hydrangeas (3 flowers each)
- 3 Stems (white) cosmos (4 flowers each)

Tools

- Wire cutters
- Yard stick

Instructions

1. Wedge foam into basket and cover with moss. Secure the moss with floral pins.

2. Cut four boxwood stems to 12" and insert two straight up on both sides of the handle and two on each of the ends. Cut the remaining stems to 8" and fill in the basket.

3. Cut four hydrangea stems to 9" and place one on either side of the handle in the center and one on each side of the basket. Cut eight stems to 8" and distribute them evenly throughout the greenery. Add the hydrangea foliage around each flower.

4. Cut three cosmos stems to 11" and the remaining stems to 7". Place them throughout the basket in-between the hydrangeas. Add the cosmos foliage.

HANGING GARDEN

Materials

- *1 (Natural) 12" vine wall basket*
- *Floral foam*
- *Sphagnum moss*
- *7 Stems (yellow) large snapdragons*
- *7 Stems (orange) California poppies (with buds)*
- *4 Stems (purple) cosmos (4 flowers each)*
- *4 stems (green) ivy*

Tools

- *Wire cutters*
- *Yard stick*
- *Serrated knife*

Instructions

1 Cut foam to fit snugly in pocket of basket and cover with moss.

2 Cut the snapdragon stems to 19, 15, 12 11, 11, 14, and 19". Insert the first three lengths facing up into the foam. Bend the bottom three inches of the next four lengths into right angles and insert them into the foam facing down.

3 Cut the poppy stems to 12,10,7,9,10,14 and 20". Insert first four poppies facing up and the remaining three facing down.

4 Cut two cosmo stems to 13", two to 9" and the rest to 8". Insert the cosmos in-between the other flowers.

5 Fill in the arrangement with the ivy stems.

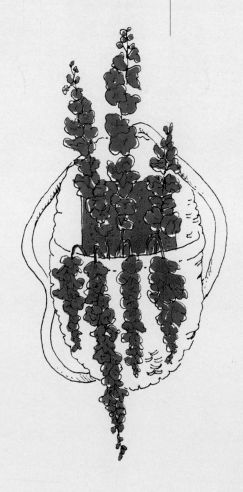

36

Fireside Florals

Materials

- 1 (Country blue) 18" basket with handle
- 5 (Oak) 16" fire logs
- Sphagnum moss
- 5 Stems (blue) large agapanthus
- 4 Stems (gold) black eyed Susan (3 flowers each)
- 1 Bush (variegated) 10 stems needlepoint ivy

Tools

- Wire Cutters
- Yard stick
- Hot glue gun/glue sticks

Instructions

1. Stack wood to extend 6" above rim of basket. Tuck the moss into the ends of the basket and in-between the logs.

2. Cut one agapanthus stem to 10" and the rest to 6" long. Hot glue stem tips before inserting throughout the basket.

3. Cut the black eyed susans into single flowers. Cut three stems to 8", three stems to 7", one stem to 10" and the rest to 5". Hot glue around the agapanthus.

4. Cut the ivy bush into 16" pieces. Cut one stem to 10", four stems to 6", and leave the remaining pieces 16" long. Hot glue throughout arrangement.

FLOWERS AND APPLES

Materials

- 1 Oval (blue) 16" basket with handle
- 2 Floral foam
- Sphagnum moss
- 1 Bunch (navy blue) ting ting (40 stems)
- 10 Stems (yellow) small sunflowers
- 7 Stems (burgundy) larkspur
- 4 Stems (blue) anemonies (3 flowers each)
- 3 Large (red) apples
- 2 Sprays (variegated) boxwood (3 stems each)
- 3 Stems (orange) tubaglia

Tools

- Wire cutters
- Yard stick
- Hot glue gun/glue sticks

1 Wedge the foam in the basket and cover with moss.

2 Cut half the ting-ting to 22" and insert in a clump behind the handle in the back left corner. Cut the remaining ting to 18" and place in a clump in the center in front of the handle.

Instructions

3 Cut the sunflower stems to 28, 26, 25, 21, 20, 17, 16, 15, 13, and 10". Hot glue stem tips and insert into foam.

4 Cut the larkspur to 26, 24, 23, 22, 21, 20 and 19". Hot glue the stem tips and insert in the foam.

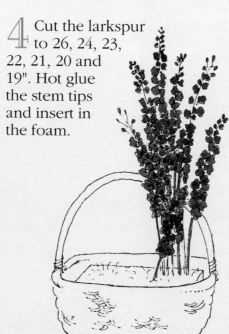

5 Cut the anemone stems to 18, 16, 13 and 10". Hot glue the stem tips and insert in the foam.

6 Hot glue two apples on the rim of the basket under the anemones, and hot glue the remaining apple to the far left rim of the basket.

7 Cut one boxwood stem to 18", and insert it on the left side of the arrangement. Cut the other stem to 15" and insert it in front of the first boxwood.

8 Cut the tubaglia stems to 15 and 12" and place in-between the anemonies and sunflowers.

SWEET CORNERS

Materials

- 4-1/2 X 4-1/2" Styrofoam
- Sphagnum moss
- Floral pins
- 1 (Green) ivy plant (16 stems)
- 7 Stems (purple) larkspur
- 3 Stems (rose) roses (2 flowers each)
- 3 Yards (mauve) #9 Moire wired ribbon
- 7 Stems (pink) freesias
- Floral wire

Tools

- Serrated knife
- Wire cutters
- Yard stick
- Hot glue gun/glue sticks
- Scissors

1 Cover front and sides of foam with moss. Secure the moss with floral pins.

2 Cut the ivy into single stems. Cut two to 10", two to 20", five to 5" and the remaining stems to 8". Establish the overall shape of the arrangement with the ivy.

Instructions

3 Cut three larkspur stems to 26", 24 and 20" and insert all three stems out the bottom of the foam. Cut two stems to 16 and 14" and insert them out the left side of the foam. Cut two stems to 10" and insert them in the center. Shape the stems in graceful curves.

4 Cut one rose stem to 9" and one to 15". Insert the longer one in the bottom of the foam, and place the shorter one above it. Cut another rose to 7", and place it above the last rose. Cut a rose and bud to 5", and place them in the center of the foam facing up. Cut the last rose stems to 9, 7 and 5" and insert the longest stem out the left side. Stagger the remaining two towards the center.

5 Cut one yard of ribbon, and wind it through the flowers. Hot glue to secure the shape. Tie a bow with the remaining ribbon. Secure the center with floral wires. Cut the wire to 3" and insert it into the center of the foam.

6 Cut the freesia to 10, 12, 14, 7 and 7". Insert them into the foam.

7 Bend a floral wire into a "U" shape and push it through the back of the foam for a hanging wire. Hot glue the ends to secure.

FREESIA
ROSE
LARKSPUR

WALL SCONCE

Materials

- 1 Styrofoam cone 14"
- Sphagnum moss
- Floral pins
- 1-1/2 Yards (tapestry) #40 wired cotton ribbon
- 6 Stems (burgundy) roses
- 1 Bush (green) needlepoint ivy (5 stems)
- 1 Stem (mauve) large hydrangea
- Floral wire

Tools

- Serrated knife
- Wire cutters
- Scissors
- Hot glue gun/glue sticks

Note: The project does not include the draped 3" sheer ribbon.

Instructions

1 Cut the styrofoam cone in half lenghtwise and cover the rounded side with moss. Secure the moss with floral pins.

2 Make a 5" wide 6 loop bow, and secure the center with floral wire. Wire the bow to the foam.

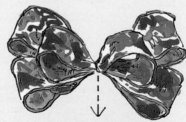

3 Cut the rose stems to 1" and insert in the foam. Hot glue to secure.

4 Cut the ivy into 3" pieces and hot glue in-between the roses and the around the bow.

5 Cut the hydrangea into 10-12 small clusters and hot glue around roses.

Note: To make two sconces, use the remaining half of the cone and double all the other materials.

Exotic Orchids

Materials

- 1 (Natural) 12" round, rattan basket
- 1 Floral foam
- Floral Pins
- Sphagnum moss
- 3 Stems (gold and burgundy) cymbidium orchids
- 2 (Natural) 6' curly willow branches
- 12 Stems (green) palm leaves

Tools

- Wire cutters
- Clippers
- Yard stick
- Hot glue gun/glue sticks

Instructions

1 Hot glue the foam to the bottom of the basket and cover it with moss. Secure the moss with floral pins.

2 Cut one orchid stem to 26" and insert into the foam in the middle of the basket. Cut the second stem to 36" and insert next to the first orchid. Cut the last stem to 22" and place in front of the tallest stem.

3 Cut one curly willow to 4' and insert in foam behind the tallest orchid. Cut the second willow into smaller branches and insert around the base of the arrangement.

4 Insert seven palm leaves on the right of the orchids, and insert two leaves on the left. Insert the last three leaves in front of the arrangement.

Note: Using your thumbs and forefingers, bend the stems of the flowers and leaves before inserting them in the foam to give a natural look.

Materials

- 1 (Dark) 12" oval basket with handle
- Floral foam
- Sphagnum moss
- Floral pins
- 12 Stems (blue and lavender) hydrangeas
- 10 Stems (yellow) tiger lilies (2 flowers each)
- 10 Stems (yellow) roses (2 flowers each)
- 2 Stems (pink) peach blossoms
- 1 Bush (green) ivy (15 stems)
- 2 Stems (Green) fern

Tools

- Wire cutters
- Yard stick

Note: Line the basket with newspaper before adding the foam and moss to avoid littering the table with bits of moss when the arrangement is complete.

Instructions

1 Wedge the foam in the basket, cover it with moss, and secure the moss with floral pins.

2 Cut the hydrangea stems from 10-12" and insert into foam.

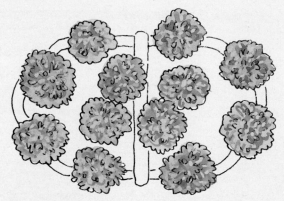

TOP VIEW SHOWING LOCATION OF HYDRANGEAS IN BASKET

3 Cut fern stems to 7" and insert in either side of the basket.

4 Cut tiger lily stems to 10" and insert around the hydrangeas.

5 Cut the ivy apart and distribute throughout the arrangement.

6 Cut rose stems to 10" and fill in any empty spaces.

7 Cut one blossom to 14", and insert in the middle of the arrangement. Cut the remaining blossom to 13", and insert in front of the taller blossom.

FLOATING FLOWERS

Materials

- 1 (Pink) 10" wall basket
- Floral foam
- Sphagnum moss
- Floral pins
- 5 Stems (white) snowball hydrangeas (3 flowers each)
- 9 Stems (rose) freesia
- 5 Stems (wine) rose sprays (15 flowers each)

Tools

- Wire cutters
- Yard stick

Instructions

1. Wedge the foam in the basket and cover it with moss. Secure the moss with floral pins.

2. Cut three snowball stems to 13". Bend the stems with your thumbs and forefingers and place one in the middle and one over each side of the basket. Cut the remaining stems to 10" and fill the basket.

3. Cut the freesia stems to 10" and insert in-between the snowballs.

4. Cut the rose stems to 10" and distribute throughout the arrangement.

Summer Fireplace

Materials

- 3 or 4 (Oak) 16" fire logs
- 20 (Natural) 48" raffia strands
- 1 Bush (variegated) needlepoint ivy (10 stems)
- 3 Stems (mauve) roses (2 flowers, one bud each)

Tools

- Wire cutters
- Yard stick
- Hot glue gun/glue sticks

Instructions

1. Wrap the raffia around the center of the logs and tie the ends together in the front.

2. Cut five ivy stems to 12". Hot glue around the raffia.

3. Remove the blooms from the rose stems and hot glue them to the logs and the raffia. Hot glue two rose leaves around each bloom.

WALL DECOR

Materials

- 1 (Natural) 8" vine wall basket
- Sphagnum moss
- 3 Yards (purple/blue) #9 French wired ribbon
- 2 Stems (periwinkle blue) bouvardia (3 flowers each)
- Floral wire

Tools

- Wire cutters
- Hot glue gun/glue sticks

Note: Project does not include draped sheer 2" ribbon shown in photo on page 55.

Instructions

1 Hot glue moss to the left side of the basket.

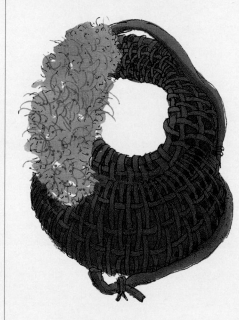

2 Make a 4" wide, 6 loop bow and hot glue it to the upper left section of the basket. Hot glue the remaining ribbon over the moss.

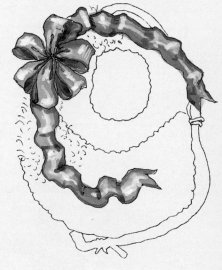

3 Remove the bouvardia from the stems and hot glue beside the ribbon alternating the flowers from side to side. Hot glue the bouvardia leaves around the flowers.

BOUNTIFUL BASKET

Materials

- 1 (Natural) 12" round willow basket without a handle
- 2 Floral foam bricks
- Sphagnum moss
- 5 Stems (gold) large sunflowers
- 9 Stems (purple) liatris
- 11 Stems (purple/lavender) delphiniums
- 10 Stems (orange) marigolds
- 7 Stems (red) anemones (3 flowers each)
- 8 Stems (yellow) September flowers (3 flowers each)

Tools

- Wire cutters
- Yard stick

Instructions

1 Wedge the foam in the basket and cover with moss.

2 Cut sunflower stems to 20, 13, 13, 15 and 15". Insert the 20" stem in the center of the basket, one 13" stem in the front left corner, the other 13" stem in the opposite corner, one 15" stem in the front right corner and the last 15" stem in the remaining empty corner.

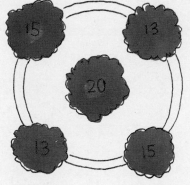

TOP VIEW SHOWING PLACEMENT OF SUNFLOWERS. THE NUMBERS INDICATE LENGTH OF THE STEM IN INCHES.

3 Insert a 26" liatris stem next to the tallest sunflower in the middle of the basket. Cut the remaining liatris stems to 22, 22, 20, 20 and the rest to 17" long. Insert with sunflowers.

TOP VIEW SHOWING LIATRIS NEXT TO SUNFLOWERS.

4 Cut three delphinium stems to 20" and insert in foam around the center sunflower. Cut four delphinium to 16" and insert them in-between the first set of delphiniums. Cut the last four stems to 15" and insert into the corners of the arrangement.

5 Cut all the marigold stems to 17" and fill in the empty spaces around the other flowers.

6 Cut the anemone stems to 14" and fill in the remaining spaces.

7 Cut one September flower stem to 19" and insert in the center of the arrangement. Spread out the branches. Cut the remaining September stems to 16" and distribute throughout the arrangement.